EC 2018

hq1

This book is to be returned on or before
the last date stamped below.

23297
Elgin

SCOTTISH POETRY LIBRARY
5 Crichton's Close
Edinburgh EH8 8DT
Tel. 0131 557 2876

STING

George Gunn

SCOTTISH POETRY LIBRARY
5 Crichton's Close
Edinburgh EH8 8DT
Tel. 0131 557 2876

Chapman Publications
1991

698413

MORAY COUNCIL
DEPARTMENT OF TECHNICAL
& LEISURE SERVICES

821 GUN

Published by
Chapman
4 Broughton Place
Edinburgh EH1 3RX
Scotland

The publisher acknowledges the financial assistance of the
Scottish Arts Council in the publication of this volume.

British Library Cataloguing in Publication Data
Gunn, George
 Sting. – (The Chapman New Writing Series,
 ISSN 0953-5306; no. 6).
 1. English poetry
 I. Title
 821.914

ISBN 0-906772-29-X

Some of these poems, and
versions of these poems have appeared in
*Akros, Cencrastus, Chapman, Clanjamfrie, Inter-Arts, Lines
Review, Radical Scotland, Voices of Dissent*
or been broadcast on BBC Radio Scotland.

© George Gunn, 1991

Typeset by Peter Cudmore at
Scotland's Cultural Heritage
High School Yards
Drummond Street
Edinburgh EH1 1LZ

Printed by Mayfair Printers
Print House
William Street
Sunderland
Tyne & Wear

23297

(12. 11. 99)
C

For Lesley

I am a traveller
trudging down
the long road
of words towards you

my true home
is the strath
of deer & eagle
of salmon & cat

but I come now
to the city
& hang the thin skin
of history there

Contents

Contents

Foreword

A poet must have ability to make verse sing, and have something to say. Without these nothing, though (s)he needs an eye as well as an ear, and some ability to think in images — not abstract; sensuous, metaphorical thinking. This seems obvious, but I see lots of verse these days by people who haven't these things and don't even know the lack. I starve for want of meat in the jaup of junk-food rowth to-day.

Not only does George Gunn's present book provide me with a meal, but a store of real chow for the foreseeable future. Here is a man aware, awake, sensible to the hell in which we live, and among all the cross-currents of a crazy world which knows the price of everything and the value of nothing, he fights back, an active, often angry suffering, against all the odds. The result is a poetry of reality deeply felt and apprehended; driving, forceful rhythms, a mountain-burn in flood. Yes, a bit murky at times not with soil but with condensed, tight-packed thought one has to unravel, refine, as it hurtles past. All of this can best be seen in the first poem, 'The Box':

> ...The tide has ebbed for you, the sting
> will heal, the songs assure us so
> your life was a glad catalogue of giving
>
> & from our like the future comes
> This is our essential invention
> & I do not believe, like Grieve
> that our brass is in the background, a sensation
>
> MacLean has shown us that our lyric has power...

You see the drive I speak of, the unique, urgent voice, the pressure of passion which is the hallmark of genuine poetry — a language too heightened for speech and demanding song. This poem alone is one of the best, most stimulating things I've read for a long time. Note too that the form is a development of the ballad measure basic to Scots poetry, and that impact of old and new which is true originality. I've often thought it could be the base of a truly heroic measure, and here the note is not only sounded but trumpeted.

Not all the poems are of this nature, of course, and he can write a clear, original lyric verse establishing beyond doubt that he has the gift of melody which is the identity of all real poetry. He is much rooted not only in Scotland but in his native Caithness, as a glance at 'Dunnet Head' will show — the ballad form again, but a new music. The pure lyric cry of Strathmore:

> The brave white dogrose & the red
> wild garlic, foxglove, the living dead
> who walk but cannot see
> this family of green beauty...

I salute a new, important voice.   *Tom Scott*

THE BOX

An Elegy

(For H.I.M.M.)

I

You lay in your first & last box & grinned
your eyes closed, your face fixed
I swear there was more than tragedy
there, & like some bedraggled disbelievers they mixed

the shadows that fell all around you as they staggered
in to see you, but not all
Some wanted to remember you as you were
as if the faller can be separated from the fall

but is any recognition possible amongst so much tea
& shortbread, the secret whisky
of a village grief curdling under
the worst gas of an out-of-date Presbytery

& where do you spin amid all this gabble
like this tired country you
slept on ridiculousness finally
& then not taking the lessons that we all are due

you slapped a silence on your own mortal acreage
as lands do now, from Ness
to Noss the broad North disappears
to property sharks & timber merchants with other cliques to bless

nurturing verdant lies which will melt from unbelieving
for we are as wetted snow before
the afternoon appetite of the Sun
What other proof must we muster when we thaw out to the core

& nail ourselves to foreign masts whose
blunt edge always faces South
like the unpacked gift of our self
delusion we punch in our coupons from fist to mouth

& all the North now is a lidless place
where junk traders come to ply
their stuff & in behind our couthy slabs
we can buy a plane that will never ever fly

Did you remember this, Helen, one morning when the wind
blew too long for your nerve-endings
when the cock crew in the lean field
where we hang our future & laugh at such precarious suspendings

but somehow I feel you did not laugh, nor ever would
again so trampled was this world
in which you had your hope
& in the distance the flag of oblivion was unfurled

It flew sometimes in other lands, where Time
had brought its noose
You left all sense inside a bath
& took your own time to set yourself loose

The faces then that came to look at you, behind
each gaze a set of compromises
stapling writs onto the tree
of possibility & then left to their own devices

they wander tamely in a numb routine, blowing
bubbles in a stillborn afternoon
they have mistaken for their lives
Sometimes those who can supply the maps sadly leave too soon

but that their leaving could be made more easy
for them we crash each door down
with a brutal ease, we are
the vandals in our own overgrown

follies. But what good is this to you
resting now in the young
end of your sentence, tickling
ultimately the thin green tongue

that will speak for all & ever
where the ice sheets meet
the sun flames, where
blindness & darkness are bright & sweet

& you now there with your name carved
on the misty mythical eyelid
of a similarly mythical Jesus who
in a torment of your wants like his flock hid

in the leather bound volumes on the Gothic
shelves where a culture that is
death bound stores its peoples'
needs, & care, like a duckbilled Platypus

on Edinburgh High Street, sits & scratches
its navel on the stone stool
of dictionaries we Scots play
a stuttering Richard to Lear's gormless fool

& when they shovel in the first spadeful
I hope we will still be alive
enough to remember that our hearts
do not close for transactions at five

& in the grass-filled dungeon where our platitudes
graze there is a nervous groping
each snout grumpingly snorting
blind in the skeleton Stalinism of our coping

But what is this need for words? The
sods are thumping steadily
onto & over all our easy illusions
& our lyrics turn to coffin nails far too readily

for now we even rack-rent time, stranded
as we are in the squalid
backwater of emotions
tub thumped into the senile complicity as valid

as any scenario where the furniture of hope
is Death, where the Old Testament
is alive & kicking, that tribal
misogyny where Force equals Government

& I quote, "Death is swallowed up in victory
O Death, where is thy sting?
O Grave, where is thy victory?
The sting of death is sin". & here I say such string

binds us tight as irons to our pathetic griefs
"& the strength of Sin is the Law"
& with such dimness we are hurtled
into the day, into the greedy bloody paw

13

of feudal slicing that plundered over
our once great *Nàbaichheachd.* Death
you are no more than another room
you are no more than a strange voice, a breath

from another weather, & when I saw your face
my own *á ghràidh*, it was my own voice
I heard, my own face there
in the black bridal clutch of that last choice

you took slipping violently into the grey
slumber that is our defeat
We have been trampled this far
but we will rise again, we have another destiny to meet

we have this world to win, we have this
singular solitude to embrace
& show ourselves, if now we can
that heroes have, & always will, wear compassion's face

But from this urge a Scotland falls
knocked senseless, blow by blow
from a mad woman's mob with heavy
hands who leave a desperation wherever they go

But then a thin hope comes to my mind
& it is Ireland's dreams
What if Hoche & his fourteen thousand
had met success instead of Winter storms

& if William Thompson's genius had transpired
to give the world an honest green coat
in which the furnace that fires every heart
would have found its measure instead of that

historical black hole in which the feeble critics
of a boot grinder's population
strive to prove the benefit
of buying & selling every Celtic nation?

Now the new breed fly in with their Bibles
& their cakes, new arms deals written
with quick drying ink, & then
with all the time it takes, the smitten

duly are smitten, never more to rise
& all their Wordsworths
& their Blakes are mere foam
washes along a poor coast's firths

& under this & more you sank one night
tranquillisers where that pulse
should be, the frozen lips
which caught this crash speak of nothing else

but even now the land you lie in, safe & strong
in the Caithness soil, womb of Gunn
& of More, sea & earth
our dual certainties, the moon & sun

of our small universe, would you now
believe that they will never
leave us to our peace
that they as pack drill's inventor

can never rest until we as a people are gone
& now other voices add to my song
We are as resistance to this intent
we will come to ourselves, at last, that long

evening of the eternal surf. The tide
has ebbed for you, the sting
will heal, the songs assure us so
your life was a glad catalogue of giving

& from our like the future comes
This is our essential invention
& I do not believe, like Grieve
that our brass is in the background, a sensation

MacLean has shown us that our lyric has power
& now love urges me close to you
We are at our best when made to retreat
but when we turn as turn we must surely do

our advance then will be to the very boundaries
of their Saxon lot
& with compassion we will resurrect
their hearts, for are we not the welders in song, hot

from the workings of our forbearance?
Ours is surely a small arrogance
We insist upon our survival
& if given, & they will surely be given, half a chance

they will do us in, so we must descend upon them
not for gaining or power's bribery
but that coronet, Grieve, is here to stay
& the cake we do not need is that of flattery

although, MacDonald, I know what you meant
You were doing what we all must do
you point out our deficiencies
with a steely hand, & the eager few

who are too eager to understand, hurtle
into the bribe so slyly offered
but a cap once doffed
is off for all time, the coin paid out is coffered

& we are none the wiser or so we think
Nana, Gran or Mither
why do your men betray you so?
So much taking has vexed our gain, what other

crowd would do it, what other mob
would imagine it possible?
Oh angel-headed monster fly
& is this raging school of waves so terrible?

But here we are, *mea culpa,* in this accentuated actuality
clipping one second off the next
& me with this damned foreign
tongue, stuttering naked, vain & wraxed

trying not to be the symphony with the missing tune
Oh but here we spit on heroes
We have mistaken reaction for philosophy
& the bigot's till still charges us up as zeroes

but we love, oh yes we love, like dry bracken
like Macneacail's poem
that is the furious truth
to be seconded to a thing unknown

Maybe we are better off, let a voice sing
Democracy, like Wolfe Tone's dreams
is wrecked now in the Republican
armada of our resurrection screams

This craggy search for resolution is damned
I know from start to finish
with garbled versions of a blotted
victory, whether heaven sent or absolutely hellish

it will no doubt ring into our ears
that we are the ridiculous repository
for an empire's disappointment
& our future's train, to them, is platform bound, stationary

I nail these lyrics to your ship's mast, poor Helen
& hope that pain like that is fenced in temporality
Oh we need that space
& tears to examine our culpability

But what you did is nothing new
for centuries we have done the same
never really knowing the reasons why
We break the rules of their aristocratic game

& there are no prisoners here, nor any alive
who would wish it so
They no longer light beacons
upon the hill, nor do they know

our exact strength, but oh Helen, Helen
your choice was not the Celtic way
brought up as you were with the gamble
of the Wick streets, who is really to say

that you were wrong, or that I am right
Form is so dismal in these terms
& the fading nervous light
is like personality manifest in insect swarms

So where does this leave us, am I
the one to point to understanding?
I think not. You bred a poet
who cares only for flight, not landing

But what end of the spectrum do you need
I hear more voices than mine saying "Selfish"
others saying "Pain", both bruisingly true
but they do not help us. This is the devilish

truth that we must face & face it soon you will
I'm crying out here from my wordy seat
that decision which wrecked
all basic references, we are all idols with clay feet

What did you expect, coupled to a farmer's boy
who thought that marching boots
were music, who wore a moustache
like Hitler's charm, & as to exploitation was in cahoots

with all the greed-raked eagles
who patrol our patch
dollar bags where their
touch should be, they clamp down batons against a door with no latch

& expect us all to be carefree
or at least as daft as they
You couldn't reconcile your
pulse to that, neither by night nor day

I imagine you slept unwell throughout all this ravel
& now it is too late for turning
Many's a witch we had in our midst
but none would thank you for the burning

& rightly so, why should they suffer
are you not one of them?
Ah, there we have it
yours was a spark in the general flame

of all those women who down the years
left us all the better for it
Yours was that ivory incantation
& now I starve here in my metaphorical garret

but that is not your fault nor this
tottering world where the blackness
that has become their favourite colour
is spooned onto the palate like a sickness

borne of nothingness & against its poisoned title
I spit but tongue-tied now I pause
like Connolly, America-
bound, thinking out his cause

I stroke the railing of this bloody
boat, Helen, where do we go
& why do we expect answers
formed as prayers from those who will never know?

Now what is love, here where patience
is so uncoming, where words
knife us to the board game
of our meaning, I ask, "What is love, what are words?"

Did the words of love turn to ashes
in your mouth, & you lay
untended, a cooled flame in the final hearth
& to have stopped so near? Oh love was only a surge away

it stalked with the moon, whispering up the tides
Love was young on Dwarick Head
Love was fresh Atlantic water over
eager backs, but not now that you are dead

II

"*Mairg an t-sùil a chì air fairge
ian mór marbh na h-Albann.*"

(Pity the eye that sees on the ocean
the great dead bird of Scotland.)

'An t-Eilean'—
Somhairle MacGill-Eain

This is the grey place where the grown men
groan from one more ridiculous
crusade, from an Assembly when
another power does say so, no plus

but a minus here, from foreign rule
whether it be the benign
fascism of a cathedral state, or cool
ruin from a dollar more lang then syne

They groan now as the slack hinge door
blows shut on the damp garden
of a people's workings, ever more
harvesting a soft crop which will ever soften

There is no one fit for the weeding here, Helen, no
no nimble hands to coaxen out
that other image of ourselves, so
that we unfree our voice & hear it shout

or ride around with "no-selfs" in Freudian armoured cars
with stolen tambourines & drums
tapping our tunes out through the bars
flagging out a ragged world where no wanton hatred comes

but still the talk is of boundaries & death
all around, preserved in battles long ago
where the led copped their last breath
& the rubble of their overlords still refuses to go

& these same lords now sniff the wind
with a bruised & tempered nose
The blin singer is now truly blin'ed
so down a Scottish tube the brave new man now goes

The woman of this deal has long since gone
but to that place he never looked
anyway, that ugly duck a swan
but then that story was only spoken & never booked

& the rotten registries of a scheming few
bedeck the shelves of a robber's library
& in those books which sketch the new
there lies the solemn print of a heavy collared slavery

& now in this place, Helen, we are like a song, or shadows
We run from ourselves, or if not
then like you we catch what borrows
itself as us, the imagination somehow furiously hot

& so, like hidden wine, we are that news
that no matter what your design
the strangeness it implies would bruise
that which will not take, the fine

features of an idiot caste. Ecosse
your knees tremble, the flak
you caught on blind men's missions will ferry
you back to places that do not recognise "back"

& if by chance we give ourselves to ourselves then it only
is to feel our own tail coat
& if borrowed shadows prove too lonely
we always have the dry side of a continent's boat

& the noise on our boat builder's roof
is that of one too many rains
& how we tarpaulin up the proof
that we now have free ankles but still feel chains

Oh but Helen, your eyes that night shed
more than light on their way
to alchemy, from one metal state it led
to another, now so it is, to calcination, no area grey

in this process, now two to putrefaction, the third
rams shut upon our screens 'the' solution
& along the razor the bird
parrots out a conjunction, a distillation

(At last, at last, we have no past
our gruntings)

To where can we run, glance glad under skies
that are all the gods we ever knew
to the still roaring Morven who lies
ice tide left on the Caithness border, too few

are those other mountains, too dark are their
peaky dreams for we are made
from sea & coastland & green air
Oh now, now, we will not fade

under that or any other landscape
We are our own creations
With cormorant & gull we gape
through the incoming tide of our aspirations

(At last, at last, we have no past
our lexicon)

21

So are we to have the art of traders, a swap shop
culture of this & that?
But in that cave the full crop
of human desire they had off pat

& on the wall, beside that need
to conquer fear, they put
the mark, our first seed
yours & mine, but now we pay per foot

for the little love life lends us
but your face is my face
& that hand, no fuss
or bother in its making, honest sand instead of lace

The first act of our understanding, our will
for a future. For then we had
no history nor need for optimism, we'd had our fill
of mythology which would drive us mad

(AT LAST, AT LAST, WE HAVE NO PAST
our language)

Helen, you took control in your way
on how we came & went
& in my grief's grasping twilight you lay
that afternoon, a life's folio, my tattered testament.

ON DWARICK HEAD

The wind is my stinging radiance, the sea
like angry marble jests with cliffs
slapping their sides & then to me
the seagulls screech a shower of "ifs"

if this place, lying like the brown back
of some still-sailing ship
would buckle now & lose its track
what good to me this wind, this grip?

but joy is young & now the Sun breaks through
the rolling prison of the clouds
are we only what we say & do?
if so, then here is only space for crowds

ah village, below me like a ragged cross
you spread yourself between the showers
& Spring above your blue roof bites like moss
& I, here too, chew through my hours

where is panic now, as from field to beach
the north wind knocks our pendulum
& like lightning flashing just out of reach
we sway & crack in our tidy Jerusalem

DUNNET HEAD

The wind shifts nothing save the sand
& that without a pause
over Dunnet Head it comes to land
& the beach gives rough applause

where is time here, it has no place
or downright claim
to say we know its face
we still survive in clusters & are the same

each tide will leave us & come again
its music awash like memory
the sea knows us better than the wind & when
she beckons to us we know no hurry

there is no high place here to raise your voice
this is an anarchist landscape
where angels learn of gales & choice
is Holborn's point or Wrath's distant cape

TRINITY

Sutherland, your name sits on the page
like a ridge of hills
my vast brown angel
how you gave me poetry

Ross, your craggy lyric in my veins
like the song of a cnoc or a scree
you are distance & space
close to the savannah of my tongue

I, a Galleach, Norse & Gael
Caithness shapes my trinity
my grand linking sisters
your power sends me ranting for justice

your people in my voice like a christening

THE FALL

(For Helen More)

Your father one day in nineteen twenty two
with two barrels upon his shoulder's fold
lost his balance on the quayside
& fell into a herring boat's open hold

& like that gone industry he fell too far
carrying too much, & later
through two cancer long years he died too soon
Wick now is dull from the ringing absence of a cooper

ORKNEY HAIRST

1

The moon is full again tonight
how her face is an orange dance
the grim waves dissolve their own insistence
the streamlined gulls caress their rock face

she is swept now, the moon, to blue silence

2

The South wind rasps at its most hungriest
like a tax collector whose lips kiss ice
the mist swirls in a drunken fleece
of zeros across the shivering crown of Orkney

3

The full moon, her night, her home
here in this sleeping dragon of stone
beneath such like as Maeshowe
there lie dreams which have as their moment

the clash of axes, a moon which shines
on Sweyn Asliefson & the song
in the lungs of his pulling oars
through the silver channel of runes

there go the raiders, to the sea eagle
of their great ambition, there roars
Sweyn Asliefson, dead in a pit
in Dublin, his eye bright with Vikingry

HER OWN DOMAIN

Her mouth was full of honeysuckle
in darkening October
her mouth sang bath tiles
her mouth was like the tides of Duncansby

She sang her resolution, oh she sang
her resolution, large as barley fields
as solid as the cliffs of Hoy
oh her resolution, she sang her end

in October, darkening October of the rains
her song like a cyclone
her eyes shut to dusks
dawns, her eyes shut to darkness

her ears to the tongue of owls
her eyes to my blood
my skin, to the sounds of night
the language of jawbones & dust & knives

her mouth swallows continents, empires, her heart
is my green library
the ghost of sweat, the push
of resistance, her own domain

TWISTED KNEE

It began like this, I ran into John Knox, a fierce centre-half
I was coming out for this daft cross
(I was like that, a great young goalie)
it was mine all the way, but no, thump crash

The bastard twisted my knee right round
& I lay there screaming, eating grass
The trainer ran on & gave me the "sponge"
John Knox said he was sorry really, was

going to pass back, we were on the same side
Centuries later, wiser now but alas
shouted at for staying on my line
I did my Italian goalkeeping, an elastic mass

of arms & legs leaping, punching, deflecting
"He's a guid keeper, bit frichtened o' the cross"
they said. Undeterred I soldiered on
with clean sheets & magic reflexes, the boss

between the posts, John Knox unfortunately became
team manager (now we never even won the toss)
we were stripped out in black, lost heart, skill
We all developed twisted knees, & alas

were relegated to the second
division, for ever, amen

DEATH OF A HIGHLAND WOMAN

From this ungainly procession of attentions
she did not go clean
two weeks of death's intentions
lay like burning irons in her leg full of gangrene

eighty years of the matriarchic, not morphine, cooled that agony
& made her know she would never again
walk with her baking through to the scullery
her new girdled half-yokin for hungry harvesting men

but that was between the wars, the last
which we now call the First
& the Second, for us the recent past
she had a farmer's knowing way to slake a dry thirst

her heart still a Gael, a dark Bralbin Gunn
they drifted back east as the century turned
homeward to more than
croft & the dark Greenland[1] earth others had spurned

they invented then what they did not know
& made the sand retreat
they were a dour bunch, as slow
& purposeful as each day another impossibility to meet

so what had she done to be wracked like this?
each breath, toward the end, a knife wound
a living hell has its own kind of bliss
but then the sounding bell of her life hit its final sound

& she in her ending's wave storm was cast
onto the last barren shore
when all that has come is past
& where her pain would be her crucifixion no more

1 Greenland is a district of Caithness roughly between Dunnet and
   Castletown.

THE NEW KLONDYKERS

(For N. Christie More, my Grandmother)

Come Christmas the only link between Ullapool
& Bulgaria is mackerel, so fidgeting
on the upper deck of a MacBrayne's ferry
we looked out at them still & low, sitting

on the blue shimmer of Loch Broom's edge
fat, productive & rusting like the burnt
out shell of some abandoned idea
steel chrysalis holding out the old economic hunt

for some two thousand just like you, trooping off
with your cousins each distant
summer to Lowestoft, Falmouth
Grimsby & hereafter, gutting your way to an instant

poverty, prolonged until the sea's reluctance
became a human failure
& again there is a certain hysteria
as local boats off-load, we know now a seizure

as gripping & implausible as Gàidhlig on the clipped
vowels of Russian tongues
we breathe in deeply & then sigh out
the oxygen of repetition from our protesting lungs

FAT MAN ON A BICYCLE

It was one of those fine bright mornings
that only June can bring
to the far north, & he peddled
through the turned in village
sniffing the cut salt air
as it blew in off the sea
thinking his thoughts of peat-banks
& silage, of how the clipping
would go that day & about the beer
as his brow shone like a moon
from his efforts & the hurried porridge
his breath like kettle steam before the boil
his legs a slow manx wheel
the sun caught his promise as he passed

IN THE LOW LAND

In the low land, in the far North
there sleeps one who gave
her eyes & all her worth
to sea & land & that vast thing called love

where does she dream now, now that
her nights are liquid & the substance
of her blessings is what
any poet would call her memory, & its insistence

to go back to her now, what words
could I say to her & she to me
remorse is not distilled from verbs
& anguish is a thing we can never see

31

THE QUEEN MOTHER DRIVES
THROUGH DUNNET 1968

The gouchy bitch now striven small
turns the corner from
one decade to the next
The haunting voices she leaves behind
      form & duplicate

Early morning howling wind through window
ghostly shredded wheat of stuff
small & getting smaller
I, cropped head, young & daft

bleary-eyed, red-lipped & ruddy
stared crudely, still & bronze
Her hat, her hat, oh like
a cake universe, so ridiculous

I loved its fabulous presence
& her coat so dead
& strung, the unlovely
metal swish of car, of power

Her landrover cavalcade because up here
we are slightly rough
This is not quite grouse
country but we are surely slaves, alas

it rumbles through the little village, glinting & dumb
slumbering & skulking under the
Atlantic sky, our flat parallels
Uncaring she rides past, oh wicked mother

I was mucky shoe'd & far too shy
to whisper, bow & arrowed
a peeping red skin behind
an all-too-Scottish hedge

My arrow was not aimed at you
lady of another time, oh no
but at the sun
the big egg we hardly saw

for we were not about to pull down France
& lay Chicago low, oh yes
these were itchy times
The splattered moment every year you poured
              through here, we did not care
                    pale, peat-eyed & rigid-faced

we watched the ugly thump of monarchy
parade its ghastly airs
Unusually succombed some laughed
& waved, the sea soft cheeks a mass of doubt

in curious amazement at such a drouth
of meaning, a congregation
of point & gape with faces broad
& elemental, eyes blurred & unknowing

on something strange & mistaken
a visitor from another time
of when she cleared Kildonnan
& Strathnaver for it was she as sure
              as the Duchess of Sutherland

or the Duke, they plodded down
to coast or hell
& now she smiling
waving back, a gesture from a Rolls Royce
              does not right this diurnal wrong

Mackay & Gunn & Sutherland, place-names
of a people's ghost
hang stubborn on Canadian
Australian, Kiwi, Yank, but we forget

as if this is forgiveness built from time
but in my heart
I do not forget
for in *bliadhna na losgaidh*[1] or 1968
    a crime is still a crime

but with a wave & a smile & fur coat
& a chauffeured life
of castle & wealth
the money'd bric-a-brac of the robbing elite
    she blusters past

I hung my bow & arrow over my back
& walked the starry miles
to Dwarick Head
to listen there to my anger fly

& swoop out, out to the Atlantic
that tearful ocean, I let
my arrow that was more
than mine retrace that ancestral route

but she, unknowing, motored onto Mey
& there in the bay beneath me
fat & ridiculous, anchored
by Scrabster's smiling side, grinned

        the Brittania

1   "The year of the burnings"

EAGLE & CROW

(For Morris Blythman 1919-1981)

Eagle & Crow, Morris, are among us now
with treaties on their platters
they star in that familiar show
of memory & how it matters

the perspective in which things are remembered
this is the law of democracy
for the newly interred
how far we remember is how far they say

war is peace & peace war
the mirror is Eagle, Crow
they take our language where
we never meant it to go

brave Eagle, brave Crow, our commentators'
words are fuel for the furnace
a fresh sword of reason for the gladiators
a strap of thorns for the war horse's harness

Johnnie Staundstill is their favourite man
his shoulders sag heavily from paper accords
his eyes are a twin television plan
of how we can be made to love these cruel birds

POEM FOR THE GILLE MOR

They soak up the soil
around you

the money beetles
sweating their rust

out into the air
like killer algae

they devour all nutrients
negate all life

but eventually
nature needing no prisoners

they destroy themselves
& are swept back out

into the levelling sea
but the money beetles

they have misunderstood us
for our hearts

are like the moon
sailing through

the green blood of Strathmore
our freedom as yet

a sweet cloud
& the promise of rain

hail, gille mor
your breath

is no whispered anthem
your tongue

is no quiet flag
sing, gille mor

sing of Scotland
& the world

& our names on it
for have we not heard

the itchy taunting
of a Caledonian *cante jondo*

your voice
has no darkness in it

your pibroch, gille mor
is like the dawn

with sunlight approaching
mar riutsa tha m'irisleachd[1]

oh what need have we
of the money beetle

[1] "with you my humility"

HELLO, JAN PALACH

Hello, Jan Palach
how are the dreams of the angels?
do you wear your
inferno like hair?
hello, Jan Palach
now that the years
have brought you home
& your burning star
shines above the doorway
to the Czechoslovakia
of your heart

Who pushed Jan Masyrik
through a bathroom window?
"The truth will out"
he told the UN
the feet of Jan Masyrik
followed him to death
& the teeth of Stalin
stonily grinning
like the Elgin Marbles
in the mouth of a whale
silent to truth
immune to questions

Hello, Jan Palach
August now is ripe
your red song
has refound its tune
the melody is building
the music comes like rain
incessant like love
like the laughter
of children
deafening the dull
motor sound of tanks
of armoured cars

It has put the dew
of aspiration
onto the expectant
lips of a regenerated
people, a hopeful crowd
raw like fire
swift & beautiful
like the wind
we shall see
Jan Masyrik walk again
& the burnt body
of Jan Palach heal

HAPPY BIRTHDAY, ANTONIO GRAMSCI

Here where young stags rut & gather
where tambourine & guitar rattle
setting rubbish up as culture
& transatlantic accents prattle

your cool tones & truthful reason
reach me even in this electric sea
this bedlam of a failed season
you cite the failure & I am free

free to laugh & love my prison
brick by brick I tickle it & when
I no longer hear the derision
this will be the time for honest men

but honest men are cripples now
(happy birthday, Antonio Gramsci!)
your words can show us how
to look at visions & learn to see

they couldn't stop your brain, no
they couldn't lay the head of silence
down on your prison pillow, no
your life & work is another chance

to reconnect the 'us' & 'them'
to open our mouths & sing 'I am'

FIFTY YEARS TOO LATE

(For Federico García Lorca 1898-1936)

The wind slashes the thin drape
we always knew as morning

the tide has slid in & out
since urgency washed itself into my memory

the day is rested upon a thin stave
I recognise as useless

but what need you of this, Federico, your songs
are like the fulmar's screech

as they do battle among the sandstone crags
oh Lorca, no wave will reach you

no sea can calm you & only in those dry Arizonas
do you water the brittle tubers of daybreak

AN AFTERNOON IN AUGUST

(for Patrick Kavanagh)

A blather of butterflies getting drunk
from blue flowers, flowers
surrounded by fields of wheat
the Sun blazes through her hours
& a tree caresses its trunk
& tickles the world at its feet

the machinery of harvest drones on
& the plumes of burning chaff
fill the blue August sky
a rabbit makes a grouse laugh
she whips the air that she has won
this is the time to live & die

& into this a man must come
carrying the many headed monster
of his art & the trouble in its making
& like the ancient bards of Ulster
he should sing of butterfly & of Sun
instead he checks his hands, they are shaking

RIVER IN SPATE

(for James Connolly)

Run river run for James Connolly & his memory
run for Ireland & Scotland, their history & their misery
take all those crashing trees
take all those restricting boundaries
run & sing for James Connolly
run river run, from the sky
crash reason through this land
be a searchlight, be a beacon
oh river run for us all
starving as we are, here on your dangerous banks
river you are our blood
river river you are laughing glad
for James Connolly, for that bullet
through his shirt, who did they kill
then that day, & who are we
oh river do we listen to your song
forge your course, as you must
you are your course, & we are yours
running river run, your natural anarchy
sing sing for James Connolly
sing for Ireland & Scotland, their history & their misery
& if we die, as die we must & surely will
let us have your freedom singing brightly
you are the wine of our freedom
Ireland, Scotland, run river run
until our freedom is won,
today we sing of James Connolly

CARGILL'S LOUP

(For Hamish Henderson)

Wild toe'd like the Devil
you must've been
& just like him
in one hell of a hurry

Donald's loup, you ran
& jumped across
the Ericht's frothing pow
whipped up between rocks

the brown & white gargle
down from Glenshee
you flung yourself
astride it & landed where

in the Blair of the Roman battle
your menu boiling
like a pan
your toes in your earholes

one side of which cooks in Perth
a green undulating pun
the other bank simmers
in southern Angus dreams

& along Strathmore you took
your buggered bible'd
argument & fled
to death among your remnant

but here in the Ericht now
are boulders & bowling
water, as slick as nature
over black mossheads of snakes

caught in stone & fins
of giant reptiles stuck in rock
the river is the gear
of all the engines of the hillsides

& from which to which comes an argument
laughing like a no-no theology
dancing its sound pride
& there for Scotland you jumped

a Presbyterian swimming in space
while thumping Stuarts
clawed up their bile
& maybe now you could never land

from Scotland to Scotland you louped
Donald of the Ericht's roaring
of all that could never
have you coughing in a distance

like the sick sheep of half-thought improvements
Donald your feet are huge
like Angus, like Perth
or the swab scrape of Glenshee

this is the bladder, the bowel
the lung of your purpose
from the Gàidhealtachd to the Tay
we flow our stormy breath away

where could you land, Dhomhnal Cargill
the banks shifting as you fly
& did you curse them then
the ugsome dragons of Claverhouse & Dalziell

or like a kind of Christ did you tickle their nose
astride this sculpture
of a river, still
Cargill, you forgot your books

the river wants them by night
by day, by the ink
that is volunteered by the trees
the paper is the spy's own skin

oh Cargill, the dog of nonsense bit at your balls
from plane to plane
to insomnia, Donald yes
but you leapt across with nothing

you leapt across to the Knoydart of the reclaimers
you landed in the Somme trenches
you crashed like Buster Keaton
onto the crossbenches of a dying parliament

oh yes you landed, like a weather forecast
on the tongue of Gerry Adams
you flew like dew
onto a leaking nuclear reactor

the river, Donald Cargill
is the angry wine of death
your unwanted Rubicon
where they read of crossings in your palm

& now night slid in between
your thighs, Cargill, aye
& Scotland sex'd itself
like a dog against a fence

& the priests of Cromwell upon your hat
& that ridge of nettles
along which you danced
an epileptic in Blairgowrie

& did you land, Donald Cargill
in the place you wanted
dreaming of hymnaries in mid air
& of a state that could never exist

PULLING POTATOES

Young girls on a bridge
jeans, love bites, blonde hair
boys cat-calling from outside
a chip shop swathed in grease
in any town, in Angus
some forlorn figures
by a closed pub in Summer
cars parked in the square
a bus, recently passed
causes conversation, it's late
the girls have nowhere to go
the boys will show them
how to pull potatoes instead of heaven
& how the dancing corn is cut

RHUBARB

A cash crop, they stand among it
machete in hand, a group of them
ferried as a team from Dundee
in a rusting blue bus which waits
as they truncate the sour red stems
leaving the leaves to form
wrinkled green teepees under the sun
hoarding up their poundage
as the farmer clinks his eyes
A child, tired inside the heat
plays despite himself with a paper bag
sitting like a slow pink doll
uneasily in the blood coloured stubble
& the air thick from rhubarb

THE BERRY FIELDS

The blue sky sings its oceans down
the berry fields, the berry fields o Blair

the emerald acres island in the town
the berry fields, the berry fields o Blair

here is Ericht, Sidlaw, Strathmore
the berry fields, the berry fields o Blair

the green fields greet the wheatfields tan
the berry fields, the berry fields o Blair

wisdom is the sleeping man
the berry fields, the berry fields o Blair

when the night whispers silver from the moon's set pilgrim
the berry fields, the berry fields o Blair

the wood pigeon winds poetry around her children
the berry fields, the berry fields o Blair

from Alyth's square to Coupar Angus
the berry fields, the berry fields o Blair

no disputation will come among us
the berry fields, the berry fields o Blair

here with elder, dogrose & red fireweed
the berry fields, the berry fields o Blair

of aggravation we have no need
the berry fields, the berry fields o Blair

so nature's flow does shine & broaden
the berry fields, the berry fields o Blair

see the morning forge her skyline golden
the berry fields, the berry fields o Blair

see the blue sky sing its oceans down
the berry fields, the berry fields o Blair

the emerald acres island in the town
the berry fields, the berry fields o Blair

THE BERRY HARVEST

The big black corbies hang like exiled bishops
above the blood red eyes of the berry hedges
& the Sun seeks its sleep in the cradle of the hillsides
where the stumbling hare rolls her eye in a puddle of delights

& in the mushroom ring of shabby caravans
the deep dozing pickers fill their dreams
with warmer days & better deals
& the snoring farmer with a new wife & silver tractor wheels

WHEAT FIELDS

The strath lies in blue mist
as thin as argument
as cool as reason
the trees whisper their Autumn song

the fields around me like seas, the new bales
sit like some bad joke
& the recently cut wheat fields
leave their straw to be frowns, waves

& yet without suffering & death
nothing can be learned
O Saurat, I hear the hungry roar
of an American tractor, the geared approach

of blades, of machines which tie & package
some gulls veer off in useless panic

NINE LYRICS FROM STRATHMORE

1

The brave white dogrose & the red
wild garlic, foxglove, the living dead
who walk but cannot see
this family of green beauty

2

& now the moon ducks behind the clouds
& rainbows hang onto the day
who could not love these sweet placings
oh, you Sidlaw Hills, you sing of love & that we may

3

The brave white dogrose & the Red
wild garlic, foxglove, the Strath's bed
is made, oh river, your silver word, your language bled
now the blind man leads the led

4

The wild peas form a green cream starred
hedge in front of my eyes
behind purple lupins the broad throat
of Strathmore sings the ancient heart of Angus

5

Here is the yellow flower of the whin
see it, that perfect colour
how it reminds me of you
how the shoals of memory swim to you

6

Who are you, listener, hearing these
sad verses from the glad smile
of Strathmore, all you can know
is that love lies beyond these hills, these verses

7

Tell me your story, Strathmore, oh yellow heaven
is this the truth? the orange
flame which is your tongue
you are broad & shifting, this must be the geology of courage

8

You are swimming through the heart
of Scotland, Strathmore
you cannot govern us, you cannot
imprison us, your quilted shoulders heave

9

The tears of morning tell us that
we must swim & when you grin
our river boils, & it cannot be
oh heaven, let the earth in

THE BATS

Little dark birds of night
the bats flick & spittle
under the sycamore tree
their hearts blip through
the radar of their love
feeding on the insects of the dusk
these tiny geometries
chart their bodies
across the evening of their joy
now that the night is dreaming
of her sister, the morning
the ecstatic bats are turning moths
to bats & to silence
& the night will hold them
free in her velvet arms

SONG OF THE POST-WAR GENERATION

You lie like storm blackened wheat, field after field
of you, damaged, forgotten by the harvester
a harbour for crows, ravens, gulls
the defeated generation we look back upon

without the life wound of the blade, the sacrifice
was it just the weather of the consumer
or the enormous task, the urge to production
which undid you? Now we can never hear your song

buried & cast in the clay soup of soil & mud
your bones turned over by the disrespectful plough
& our dogs will sniff & abandon them
& in your houses the silverfish swim in the dampness of absence

& from the red tunnel of your justice & vanity
younger sets of eyes look to us with vanishing charity

FOOL OF ALBION

One night when the moon was halved
& all the sky was green
I took my love to a distant shore
to a place she had never been
I cried "Blow you summer winds blow
& let your piper play
& when your tune is over
then we'll marry on that day"

we waited for an answer there
my own true love & I
hoping for a blessing to come
down from that bottled sky
but not a single word we heard
not a sound nor any sign
except for our anxieties
which were jangling in a line

my love she cried "I'm cold now
my hands are thin & blue
all I hear is the laughing sea
& my love it laughs at you
oh take me to a secret place
we can call it Babylon
& let the light hide you from my face
fool of Albion"

& with nothing more than a whisper then
into a bird she turned
& flew through the green dark sky
into the moon which burned
all trace of her into its missing half
like the furnace of the Sun
& I returned to the morning
as dull as I had begun

oh where is hope now, where is hope & all that I desire
lost in moon & sea & sun & smoke & mist & fire

DON'T GO TO GLENEAGLES

Champagne dolls, cynocephali, fur coated
on their wadded way to Gleneagles
golf! luxury! fascist deals bloated
up in plumed lounges where the brandy & cigars
 yell rich rich rich death-head!

lipsticked, like horses bridled, rank equerry
they flock to where-ever, it's not Scotland
Scotland, that disused mining camp of bars
lurching half drunk in the sough of history
 it's not here, sterling unitors!

it's not here, we walk on dead men's heads
stilletto in the eye, don't go
to Gleneagles, no! mascara
craven & derelict, don't think, so
 don't go, suntanned tiara newly weds

money bleeding from every ear, they laugh
out the window, they laugh at Scotland
out the window "Are those houses?"
"No!", "Really" lips, teeth, tongue, gland
 necks giraffe from saffron blouses

"It's really quite different up here, isn't it" out the window
of the train, they laugh & want
French cigarette smoke frilled out
like peacock feathers, Italian luggage, a fashioned pant
 they go to Gleneagles, please don't

rich wives of even richer men, why?
they go to Gleneagles, why?
haircuts costing more than any
thin state benefit, they go to Gleneagles, why?
 they go because they are not many

the ghosts of raccoons & beavers yell
in their ears "Don't go to Gleneagles, or we get rough
(their comrades' pelts drape over
massaged shoulders) please don't go, go to hell
   & if you stay there long enough

your spirit may become our one bow tie!"
their eyes don't see things when they are moving
they strip the image from every object
peeling the wealth for the sake of whatever (who's to ask why?)
   wall to wall income tax avoiding

dung idle reason they condescended to look
in the first place & in the second place
they've forgotten why they are going (& this no dodge!)
to Gleneagles (don't go) but they will, & at a pace
   to that glorianna hunting lodge

where ghillies learned to whack a white pea
around some imported bloody
sand dunes while the rich men bent on venison
oiled their rifles & queen Victoria sat en-plump
   beside an ever dying stag of Ossian

& all their imagination's nothing more
than a gangrene-greased swimming pool
where the vomit gatherers learn to relax
& the metropolitans their feet do cool
   with their credit cards stored in sacks

O Africa! O Amerigo! O Asia! your blood
& bone I swear there sits
gouged & tapped by these vampire bats
perfuming their axe needy necks on socialist trains
   in a small country that is their last resort,
     we shrink our brains

Saville Row, you nipped the bud of Michaelangelo
crossed legged & humpy, don't go, we're not your sort
don't go to Gleneagles, don't go
don't buy anything, don't say anything
    we hear your horn player blowing mort

it's your plastic money'd boarding school voice
don't go to Gleneagles, oh please don't go!
there is snow on the mountains, yes, snow!
& they say that it is coloured orange
    all the way from the Sahara!

(don't go to Gleneagles!) Africa, Africa
we all came out of Africa
not on a Sultan's carriage
but hungry, wandering, changing
    jaw shape, heads (not mascara!

what has this got to do with anything
in Gleneagles?) don't go, I sing
there is a palace & in this palace
there are many things, rich rooms with exquisite
    wall hangings, extravagant toilets for the
        hard of phallus!

Swiss water feet warmers, Swedish electric duvets
& tangerine Turkish ivory nose
moisturising units (only available to élite
platinum plated card carriers!) & those
    other little essentials shipped in under plain covers
        from Paris, we are discreet

O the white skinned race is doomed, unless…
don't go to Gleneagles, don't go
not on this train, the guy who tried
to sell you coffee, his grandmother died
    of a broken heart in a damp tenement in Glasgow

her family from West Sutherland displaced & missing
& bloody imperial feet all tweeded out
stamped over her vegetable garden, hissing
this & bloody that, shooting at
    imitation Japanese deer, oh shout!

don't go to Gleneagles, go to Glasgow!
do homage at her unmarked grave
prove your heart is not a chocolate
turd dropped from the arse of the Tsar, go, go!
    not to Gleneagles, it's far too late!

don't go, please don't go, not now
not on this train, not today
not until they've re-hired all the paid
off parlour maids & garni chefs *de facto*
    but in Gleneagles it will never be so, or so it's said

not until all your money, like the tears of Ra, burns
not until the Free Kirk & the Sunday Post
dive with joy into the simmering sea
& rise at Gleneagles with a crown of thorns
    that fits only you, only me

PETERHEAD

The prisoners dance on the roof
the glad prisoners, the honest men
they are our true heroes
praise them, praise them
sing of their bravery, pray for them
to your fat staff clutching banker God
hallelujah joyously in your
real stained glass prisons
hang your afterbirth on the altars
& watch those prisoners dance
give them your names
give them the reasons you spit
tell them they are holy
they dance for you

AMAZONS

In a Manhattan movie house
where there is nothing no one allows
on 42nd Street in the dim shadows
(it is a place where no one going goes)

I saw a film about the Brazilian jungle
the destruction of which is no government bungle
but instead a greedy plan
to enrich the white skinned man

an armed band were chasing this Indian boy for sport
they were bounty hunters of some sort
eventually they shot him & to prove the superiority of North
                                                          over South
they macheted off his penis and stuck it in his mouth

59

BOUNDARIES

Until all boundaries we remove
no light for us can shine
we sacrifice what we can't yet prove
to dictators, unscrupulous, benign

but what proof is needed except that pulse
that drives us to our fate
without the dragnet of convention's curb
we have no borders, it is never too late

but yet what else should humans need
that they cannot so attain
it is the meaning of the seed
& the rhythm of the rain

POEM WITH THE WORD ELEPHANT IN IT

Uncurable thirsts
& everything comes quickly

the dry throat
& the words of the tribal song

a torn list of religions
& groceries

a bus ticket to a city
by the sea

like this a man will always
choose a bicycle

in preference
to an elephant

WOLVES

Wolves once roamed these hills, bears slept
heavily in the stark ravines
what language then did they speak
these nervous cave dwellers who before my eyes

now parade, setting testing feet on rusted
taxi cab roof, who make urgent hammers
out of park memorials, baronial window
surrounds, who fish with redundant radio aerials

the still mucus pools of the river, what
time echoes them back when all
who now so certain in their living
will have drunk the green draught of death's family

& will mingle with them, invisible, tongueless
dragging the habit of chattels
waking bears, startling wolves
with the ugly clanking of their terminal obsessions

the horizons that they occupy are those
of whispers, & they take
their dictionary from the sun
& grow wheat where the motorway submerged

TITANIC

1

I opened the door & went abroad
whupping up & down the country
like a zipper, achieving what?
groaning like an open cast mine

the wound of my mouth, another place
I could never return to & is it true
we can make too much noise?
I don't believe it, probably never will

jimmied as a puddle of trees
like a curdling rough field
some farmer has rubbed back
with his teeth & shoved a loud curse

into its brown thankless belly
we survive in trouble, our looks
are journeys, a signpost
tells you you are home & yes

they clack at you in their fashion
& their faces fit the sounds
the pink thrapple of language
the only door I could really open

2

His head is full of dreams & anger
his heart is full of songs & fury
        anger & dreams
        fury & songs

we have German roads built with English paper
& the beautifully photographed lie
of dockyard cranes, tenement facades
& the public poetry of a newspaper hack

what have we become? a surge
of cannibalistic sheep, half drugged
& mauling the green grass of somebody
else's home, less green, less homely

the Titanic, as brave a rivet job
as ever Belfast shat smacked
a pop-up iceberg, sank like a tin of spam
the arch-angel Gabriel tooting on his moothie

as from the hold wailed boredom boredom boredom
"We haven't paid all this money
to be fucking killed" as if death
could wait until after dinner, it won't

it took hold of the table cloth of that trip
like a mischievous child & threw
it into the air, messy
like a roughneck's party, or chocolate

3

The well-manicured jealous dog of reason
yelped like a hiccup
& John Bull kicked its arse
blundering out stories of dynamite & glue

who'd be a bully's mange? there are rows
& rows of them, these uptight sentries
at the mouth of the comic cave
we put up with twaddle & are known to grin

the furious dreamy songs of anger
& what is that accent anyway
nobody really speaks like that!
she slept with a paratrooper & did it campaign style

she stopped the traffic alright & he drove
a butch green jeep along the track
of her thin young body, she dreams of snow
on the hills, of fish, of the smell off her grandfather's pipe

the rattling punch club of domesticity
& how it stank, looking on sex
as socialism for two, or more
depending, outside the door that jealous dog

(For the 167 dead of the Piper "Alpha")

My eyes are rivers of fire
& the dead feed on my chorus
on the smoke of a billowing column
on the applause of the bacon smellers
glad that they have not become
the plastic waft of melted hard hats
drifting over the gentle Summer sea
filled now with the black blood
of engineering & the fragile idolatry
of an unthought taking
    I see human tissue
turn to gas screaming its tune
of dolorous thanks through the twisted
rig legs & derrick girders flicked like pins
at the two handed dumbshow of finance & metal
& the dead sink in the neutral water
so many dead it is hardly bearable
they are at home now in the place of their origin
they fill my voice with their angry song
they sing
    "Fuck you, mate
fuck you" from under the feature pages
of middle-brow papers
list after list like nineteen fourteen
roughneck & roustabout, crane-op & cook
name after name in numbing insistence
singing
    "Back in Buchan the barley is turning
in Scotland now the Summer is green"
    My eyes see the hush-up shape & begin
from within Texan lawyers' attaché cases
it flies out, like a soul, at press conferences
like an invisible smog it both disappears & is seen
paving the way for back handed pay-offs
taking a loan of misery & grief

64

losing the place while we all watched
grown men confidently hoping that Red Adair
in his red asbestos longjohns
would ride out from the sunset
rewind the movie & make it OK
    This then the dream world of industrial oil
night after night it gets worse
the hush-up has swollen
to the size of Tehran
they park their Cadillacs in sinister places
& watch the sky burn like a torch
between the broken arms of the flare-off booms
holding the horizon still
for the many camera crews
so that we can all ooh & aah
feeling pity in our armchairs at the TV news
    I, a roughneck, tell you this
from the strange country of disbelief
the dead are always with us
we remember the dead

CUTTING

I slash & burn through words
an autumn fire upon the hill
my pencil a tusker
doing its work in reverse
laying out narratives like dry peats
a dark mixture of fear & faith
to be stacked or ploughed back in
into my skin, into the yawning
bucket ever hungry for my work
I clutch at the mire
this fertile mess of tensions
& whisper to the friendly flames
of how damned I feel in this tough agriculture
this ancient business of carving

GLASCHU

1

You're an ugly lump, Glas Chu
you slaver about the Clyde
like rabies, how I hate you
slashed like motorways
& the rising damp of poverty
City of Culture, you're
a huddled gaff of destitiutes
whacked & rammied into
cortina bricks hugging like a shadow
over a pissed-full puddle
of Gaelic evictions

2

for us you are like the Cyrenes
textile & forge
rivet & girder
Glas Chu, oh Glasgow
green place blue place
your muscled name
to Kildonan is the colour
of murder & flame
A thin slow weeping
& your face in sorrow
as I look at you now

STARLINGS

The starlings fly like a peppered cloud
held by light & space
to & fro they soar & circle
their purpose held by unknown warmth
like a small storm they
chase the perfect place to be
the feathery amoebas they imitate
& now the light has loosened
its tanned desire to harbour them
to cup their wandering in her purple hand
but she will never hold them so
for they are their own agenda & their dream
& Glasgow below them like a forgotten war
raises her nails to scrape the air

ORAN DHU

By Ben Coigach Mor, by Cul Mor
by Stac Pollaidh, by Tanera Mor
by Achiltibuie, by the restless ocean there
I heard the song of my people
of those who went by ship
down through the tunnel of centuries
remembering the song of the skylark
of the coming of Spring
& the slate world of the sea
their travels upon a stranger's tongue
how I heard them
& grew still
        By Suilven, by Ben More Assynt, by Quinag
by gull flight, by fish dream
their days as a crayon upon a page
& the tide down like nature's flag
by Stoer Point I saw their ships
by Polbain, by Altandhu, by Reiff
far from the seafields of kelp
& the hearth black from the want of smoke
westward they sailed like the setting sun
   Who will remember these then
the Vikings' child?

LIBERTY ODE

For The Gille Mor At 70

As I write this empires crumble
can I blame it all on you
Hamish Henderson?
Russia, America, cracking open
in their different ways
like an old damp Gorbals tenement
Russia, where the wild wind of freedom
blows loud at last
America, a desert of rabid dogs
& the poor sleeping beneath their feet
"All those tired old men" you said to me once
thinking of Brehznev, Andropov & the rest
& another time, surrounded by bright eyed ethnologists
you leaned across the bar & smiled, "Bloody Yanks!"
So what of our own neep patch then
Gille Mor or Johnny Tyrie
What of this peedie place
which gives us both our music & our fire
where's she bound, this girning
ubiquitous dazzle of a dame
what's Scotland's trick in Europe now?
Where on that continent's new-drawn gob
can she clap her dander & her dream?
For are we not a stravaiging rammy
of individual collectivists who cannot agree
cocking our Celtic cods
at our Sudron headache merchants
& their iron language
urging them to leave us be
& get better on their own
Ah, Hamish, they will not do it
they'll spread their clatter & cry it culture
they'll sew our arse into their Empire's thin breeks
& laugh at us circumnavigating
our own daft pivot with arguments like a broken jig

a sort of hochmagandie without the hoch
But, my friend, you know damned well
we have to ding doon our own philistines
before we can ding doon theirs
"An more's the pity" some may croak
ever ready to "wha's like us" their way
behind the tartan curtain of which you sang "beware!"
& the whole world joined in
For this country is your length
by Glasclune an Drumlochy
ye cam amang us a long shanked chiel
frae ower Cargill's Loup
a collecting man, a translating man
writing Scotland's name large
upon the page of the world
setting her talents on that maternal tongue
travelling her turf tracks of story & song
the cut peat of possibility
our stacked experience as old as that
So let the Empires fall, *a' bhalaich*
let their rotten girders go
We'll dance our tackety-booted *pas-de-bas*
like our ancestors did for America
we'll dance them into memory
& a happy past, after all, is only dust
For Empires come like the winter snow
& leave with spring's soft light
or, like autumn's yellowing leaves
they tackle eternity yet end in death
for love is change & change inevitable
This then the perfect human sea
where all sail in imperfection
for close to failure is our success in art
& our art the freedom
of which you sing

George **Gunn** was born in Thurso, Caithness, in 1956. On leaving school at 16 his various occupations since have included journalist, trawlerman, and roughneck in the North Sea oil industry.

He turned professional writer in 1983 and in 1985 was awarded a Scottish Arts Council Writers' Bursary. He has published several pamphlets of poems, the last two being *The Winter House* (1982) and *Into the Anarchic* (1985).

Plays to date have been *Roughneck* (1984), *The Poet* (1985), *Emma Emma – Red & Black* (1986), *A Cloud of Witnesses* (1987), *The Province of the Cat* (1988), *The Gold of Kildonan* (1989), *A Stromness Saga* (1990). He has also written scenes for *The Crofting Act* (1986) and for *Seen From The Law* (1990). He was writer with the Fife Local Initiatives Project between 1984 and 1986, for which he wrote a community musical called *Archie & The Aliens* (1985) as well as a video programme on the history of Methil entitled *By Coal & Sail* (1986)

...Combining intense lyricism with passionate eloquence, George Gunn's poetic voice grows in authority as it matures. Truly a poet for today.   *Donald Campbell*

...Here is a man aware, awake, sensible to the hell in which we live, and among all the cross-currents of a crazy world he fights back, an active, often angry, suffering, against all the odds. The result is a poetry of reality, deeply felt and apprehended; driving, forceful rhythms, a mountain-burn in flood.   *Tom Scott*

23297

SCOTTISH POETRY LIBRARY
5 Crichton's Close
Edinburgh EH8 8DT
Tel. 0131 557 2876